Change it!

The secrets of happiness & fulfillment in life, through change!

Amadeus Lombardi

Clink Street

London | New York

Published by Clink Street Publishing 2019

Copyright © 2019

First edition.

ISBN: 978-1-913136-82-6 (Paperback)
ISBN: 978-1-913136-83-3 (Ebook)

I want to dedicate this book to my mother, Andrea Lombardi.

She was and is always standing behind me, holding my back, and is opening thousands of doors towards my own success. My whole life, she is by my side, supported me through everything, and helped me live the life I am living now. I want to thank her for her overwhelming love, her huge heart, and her ability to help everybody. She, herself is changing lives and is helping others for a better life on a day to day basis. She is my role model and a fantastic personality. She always helped and is still helping me every day; emotionally, financially, and continuously.

Mom, I love you so much and I want to thank you for everything you have done for me. Without you, I wouldn't have come that far in my life, and wouldn't be able to live the life I am living.

"All that I am, or hope to be, I owe my angel mother."
Abraham Lincoln

Thank you, thank you, thank you.

In love,

Your son, Amadeus

Contents

Contents

Introduction

"Life isn't about finding yourself;
life is about creating yourself."

George Bernard Shaw

Welcome to the book which will change your life.

The book which has the answer to all your feelings, and which will guide you through the pain into the person you want to be.

This book helps everybody; it is not another business book, which tells you what to do; it is helping everybody to achieve what they are striving for in life. The decision to buy this book and start to read it will bring abundance and happiness to your life. Please do not stop reading it, it can give you whatever you want.

I want to thank you for buying this book, and helping me to make my dream come true, in return, I will help you make your dreams come true.

It doesn't matter if you are reading this book to reach your final life goal, if you are stuck and are going in circles, or if you want to change your life, it will help you definitely to become the person you want to be. Life is about getting help from people who can help us going steps towards our true destiny in our life. We do not need to do everything on our own, and therefore I want to thank you, for going the happy way!

Quickly to me; I am Amadeus Lombardi; I am 20 years old, and I am currently studying in London. I am not somebody who has everything achieved in life, and I will not tell you how you can earn millions or built an empire, only because I am not there yet. What I can do, is to help you on your way towards your happy life: For several years I have been studying people's behaviour, success stories, giving speeches and much more. Several times I asked myself the question; why do we sometimes have it so complicated in our life? Why are most of us not happy with the gift 'life' and why do we keep fighting it, rather than living it?

Over the years, I have spent much time identifying different unconscious behaviours we humans have. Especially the new generation I was born into. I worked on identifying the challenges we have and want to show you how you can overcome them. Other than that, I am also trying to explain you the way you think, the path you need to go to live the life you want to live. Thank you again for allowing me to share this information with you, and I am confident that it will help you in your and other people's life. I have changed my life, and so I think that with this knowledge, I can help you, to get where you want to be. I have gotten out of my alcohol excesses, which I'd had since I was 13 years old. I have left behind friends who were not good for me, and I got out of relationships which did not feel right. For everything I have in my life, I have worked. Since I was 12 years old, I have always been working and trying to make my dreams come true. I worked in the kitchen of two restaurants, filled up the shelves in a supermarket and also worked as an intern in two different companies. I moved out of my mother's house when I was 18 years old, to work for what I want in my life, and now, here I am, studying abroad at a first-class university, not letting go of any opportunities which come to my life and giving everything to have the life I am dreaming of.

This book and the following chapters will reflect what I have learned throughout my life and will show you that you can achieve whatever you want, to live the life of your dreams. However, before you can get this far, you need to understand how you can influence yourself to be able to achieve whatever you want.

When we are kids, our parents tell us we can be whoever we want. Of course, you might think, this wasn't meant honestly by our parents, but I am telling you, you can be whoever you want if you start to work on yourself, understand yourself and make yourself as a priority day by day.

You are great, we are great, and our lives are great, let me help you think the same way.

Chapter 1
What is it you want in life?

"Ten years from now, make sure you can say that you chose your life. You didn't settle for it."

Mandy Hale

While I was going through the process of writing this book the question, of what I want in my life got bigger and bigger. It is a simple question. It is built from eight words, and everybody should understand the meaning of what this question is asking, but why is it so hard for us to answer it? Why are people answering this question superficially? Why do we need to think about what we could answer?

The answer is: nobody is asking the question to themselves. I can't remember ever asking this question of anybody and getting back an honest and from the heart answer, simply because we don't know an answer to this question, which comes truly from our heart. You all are working very hard in your job, maybe you have a kid who needs attention for the whole day, you are unhappy in your job, or you are running from meeting to meeting. Perhaps you are going through a divorce, or you don't have time for asking yourself this simple question. As you have time to read this book, I would advise you to take ten minutes to close your eyes, turn off the phone next to you and all the external sources which could interrupt and think about this question; "What is it, I really want in life?"

Feel free to think about whatever you want in life. What are the changes you would like to have for a happier and more fulfilled life? Things which you might want to think about are: Do you want to have more free time, time with your kids or partner? If your job makes you happy or if you want to earn more money? Do you want to get fitter and be in better shape or do you want to be healthier and take more time for things which make you feel good?

Whatever it is, think about it and feel how your body, heart, and soul is reacting to these thoughts and dreams. Don't just think about something people want you to be or a stereotypical thought you might have. It is essential to listen to your heart and let it guide you through this meditation of finding yourself and your dreams. If you feel like you have figured out what you want in your life, slowly open your eyes and start writing it down. Write it down in detail and don't forget to describe what you have seen in your dream and felt in your heart; it will remind you of what your life should feel like. Write it down on a piece of paper and stick it against your fridge or leave it next to your bed, it should be a place you pass by at least once a day, to remind you what you really want in your life.

After this exercise I promise you, you have made a big step towards the life you want to live, and while you keep reading this book, I will bring you step for a step towards your dream life.

At the beginning of this chapter, I talked about the fact that most people do not know what they want in life and that most people don't know what their actual purpose is in this world. As I have told you earlier, I am studying in London and am taking the tube every day to get to the university and back. If you also live in a big city or are using public transport throughout your day, you should have an eye on the following; people are emotionless. Workers, students, and retired people are sitting in the tube and aren't smiling or talking to each other, the only thing you can hear is the noise of the tube, and everybody is looking sad, disappointed by life and unconscious. You might think this is because they've had an exhausting day, but the morning situation is the same, there we could say they are still tired or didn't get enough sleep, but if we really think about it, these are only excuses about what is really happening in those people's life. It is the fact that they are unhappy with their life, that they would like to have more abundance and freedom in their life, but how should they get there if they do not know what they want in life? How can they get to where they want to be without answering the question: What is it, I really want in life?

How are they supposed to get to whom they want to be, without having a clear vision of how to get there?

As you already know who you would like to become and what your life should look like, you have a massive advantage over the people who are still going in circles and don't know what they want.

As you know now what you really want in your life, of course, it takes a lot of work and commitment to get to the point where you want to be. Always remind yourself of what it is you want, and you will get nearer and nearer day by day. Please also remember to be patient, it takes time and constant work to achieve your goals. In today's world, we all want it to happen yesterday, doesn't matter if it is more money, a better job, better relationships or more free time, we need to learn to be patient and take small steps to our final goal. I am also advising you to not directly quit your job or a relationship which is not going well but to first figure out if there is a way it could get better. Give all your heart and energy to what you want and never get your focus away from your final goal in life.

Also, it is essential to figure out a belief sentence you will tell yourself day by day, or when you again doubt if you can achieve what you want. Figure out a set of sentences, which include all your goals, dreams and places you want to be in your future. Repeat it day by day and always when something lets you feel like you want to quit, let it go through your head. Remember what you really want in your life and even better, shout it out and keep believing!

The writer Diane Ackerman once said; "I don't want to get to the end of my life and find that I just lived the length of it. I want to have lived the width of it as well."

Think about this sentence; think about the meaning, and start working for what you want. Feel the effect it has on you, do you feel sad, because you already lost so much time of your life, not living the width of it? Did you even forget how it feels, to do what you want? Do you feel motivated and ready to finally change your life? Whatever the reaction is, for me, it shows how important it is, to do what you want in your life.

My mother wanted me to be a doctor because she thought it is the job you earn the most money, and it is a very safe job, as we always will need doctors in our life. I could have never imagined being a doctor, or even taking the responsibility of a human's life. I am sure; also, you did things in your life, you never wanted to do, but you did it to make your parents or friends proud or you were striving for the feeling of attention. It is human. Again, close your eyes and think about something you did for others you never wanted to do. How does it feel? Are you angry, sad, or hurt? Do you ever want to feel this feeling again?

I hope your answer is no.

Do what you really want in your life!

While you were reading the last words, I have explained how you can find out what you want in your life. However, let's get more into detail, of why it is so hard to know what you want in now-adays life?

There are several explanations of why it is so hard. Of course, the external influences play a significant role, but most importantly, it is the way we grow or grew up. Throughout our whole life, we are always treated like treasure for our parents. They always told us how perfect and excellent we are and that we can achieve whatever we want in our life. That's true on the one hand, as I believe that everybody can achieve whatever they want, but on the other hand reality is a little different. In the process of growing up, we more and more experience, how important we are. Whatever we are doing, we do not get any severe consequences. Maybe our parents took away our phone for a day, or they told you that you are not allowed to go out with your friends, but in the end, the consequences were not very serious. We more and more experience how much our parents love us, and how far we can go. We were always the most significant gift for our parents, and all the positive attention was on us. Please don't understand me wrong, it is crucial to give all the attention to your kids and invest in their future, but unfortunately, this often goes too far. After we have graduated from school, we finally are free. We feel like a big stone fell off our shoulders and think we are now free to do everything we like. The problem with understanding what we want in our life lies in the wrong understanding of life. Our parents were there for us our whole life. Whenever we had a

problem, we could rely on them; whether it is financially or emotionally, they were there for us. Now we realise that the reality is slightly different. There are so many opportunities in this world which we could use for our advantage, but we feel no support. We feel like we are lost on our path. Big companies do not necessarily care about the individual rather than on the numbers and so we feel more and more lost. We feel like we can't identify the thing we want as the instant reputation of 'you can achieve whatever you want' is overwhelming us with the possibilities which are there for us. To understand how we can overcome this problem, we need to realise that the answer lies in our heart, and that it is often enough, to close your eyes and think about your life. What is missing? What would you like to have?

It is important to make different experiences, even when they are not that nice all the time, but the answer will come to you with time and always asking yourself: What do I want in my life?

Chapter 2
What is your life's why?

*"Why do you stay in prison,
when the door is so wide open?"*

Rumi

Welcome to Chapter 2!

As you now know what you want in life, or are still working on what it is you want, you should also ask yourself the question, "Why do I want it?" Most people, especially motivational speakers and celebrities, might not answer this question or ask them of their audience. The answer to this is that it is a profound and meaningful question, whereas they don't have time to ask this question of the audience. However, it is an essential question to ask yourself when you are in the process of changing your life, getting more successful in every aspect of your life, and striving to be happier.

This question can answer all your doubts and explain your goals. This book will also talk more about dreams and goals later on but knowing your why will help you get there.

Unfortunately, most people are not able to answer

this question in a way that they listen to their heart and soul, but rather give a logical answer, to cause no confusion. An example of this might be "I want to be rich, so that I can buy everything I like," or "Who doesn't want to be rich?" which is first of all not even answering the initial question, but giving a question back, to get out of the trouble, as these people don't have an answer to it.

The process of finding out your 'why' has nothing to do with your purpose, as your purpose is what you are born to achieve or do in your life. The question 'why', will bring you more and more towards understanding your constant hunger for more, your constant desire for your dreams and goals. However, to answer this question, as already mentioned, takes a long time, time which most of us pretend not to have and therefore never will answer genuinely.

To explain a little more the reason behind answering with your head, rather than with your heart, I can assure you that this is due to the thinking we have. It is human, to always answer, to have an answer. We don't want to embarrass ourselves if we don't have an answer, and therefore try every time to have an answer ready, even if we have no idea what the answer is. This phenomenon can be seen very often, and therefore, I would like you to think about the last time you gave a solution, but you had no idea what the correct answer was.

My example is that I have asked myself so often,

why do I want to be wealthy? Why do I want to build up a company, which brings me enough income to live a good life, and why do I want to able to buy my dream yacht one day?

Maybe you have asked yourself a similar question. Your questions also might be, why do I want to have kids, or why do I want to have another more fulfilling job, or why do I want to have a better social life…? I am not saying that your question should be part of these; it is just a small example for you to understand what I mean. Your question might also be more straightforward, like why do I want to buy this or that, or why do I want him or her to be my partner? Whatever your question is, I hope you understand where I want to go with that. Everything you do in your life is based on a decision, everything. Some decisions are emotional decisions, some are logical decisions, and some are decisions which you as an individual take. It is also essential to understand for yourself and your environment, that not every decision needs to make sense for you or your friends. Every decision is a decision which an individual takes, and sometimes, I also already experienced it, make these decisions for me as an individual no sense.

There are a lot of examples you probably also already saw in your life, when something didn't make sense for you, but is it your problem, and are you the person who should change it? The simple answer is no. You are not responsible for another

21

individual's decision, and you should instead concentrate on yourself. Sometimes not everything makes sense, and this is precisely what this chapter is about.

Your own why!

As already mentioned, our life is concentrated on decisions. Some sources say that we take around 35,000 decisions every day. Imagine that you take approximately 24 decisions every minute. These decisions are not necessarily about what you are going to wear today, but about what are you going to do now? Are you going to work on our goals, or are you again scrolling for the tenth time today through Instagram and looking at the pictures you already saw trice? Are you going to give your energy towards your unique success, or again think about somebody else's decision, which you still can't understand? A decision is even something as simple as picking up your phone and texting somebody.

This is something we do unconsciously, and for sure, some of these decisions we take every day, are unconscious. However, if you think about significant decisions, you took today, can you evaluate why you took them?

For example, if you made the decision of why you contact your role-model in business? The decision of why you started to work on your goals? The decision of why you fought with your partner?

I promised you that I will help you change your

life with this book, and therefore I would like you to close your eyes, meditate, and see yourself with your why! It is essential for you to figure out your 'why', to be able to answer your why. Not only your business partners but also your friends and family will ask you this question sooner or later. Be prepared and understand yourself!

While you are taking this meditation, put all external sources, like your phone away, and take ten minutes for yourself to truly think about your why. Not only will this help to state why you are doing something, but also your mind will be more concentrated on the final goal, which is your 'why'.

At the beginning of this chapter, I told you that I would like to be wealthy one day, and also I thought that I want it in order to have a good life, give back to my family, and to be able to one day offer my children and family a good life. For sure, that's part of it, but the real 'why' is way more profound than the 'why' which came to my mind directly. Also, for you, there are different whys, some unconscious, some conscious. Your task is it to find out the unconscious ones, which lie deep in your heart and soul, and it's time for you to embrace them fully.

For me being wealthy and being a public person has much more to do with just having a good life. It is my purpose in life, to achieve significantly, and to help others. I also want to help others to achieve meaningful things, to change their life and them to be happier in what they are doing, that's why I am writing my first book, and that's why I want to use this book to raise awareness. That's one of my first significant steps towards my true potential and purpose.

But why?

When I grew up, money was always part of my life. I always had what I wanted, went traveling around the globe for at least once every year, saw the world, different cultures, and different people from young on. The negative side of this is that my life, therefore, was only concentrated on money.

My mum also helped to build up my father's career which enabled him to get more self-esteem, helped him to get stronger and to climb up the career ladder. However, I always felt that I couldn't impress my father. He was so high up, earned a lot of money, was busy all the time, and I suffered under not getting enough attention. Therefore, my heart told me that the only way to get positive attention from him and to impress him is to do what he cares most about, being successful.

Now you know my 'why'.

You might think now, that success is for your-self and not for others, or that this 'why' makes no sense, and yes, you are 100% correct.

My 'why' was so hard manifested inside of me, that for me, it was tough to change it, but this example shows you, how often we human want to impress others, without understanding that impression is something you don't need to earn, you either get form your loved ones or not – but does this make you a bad person?

No, it doesn't. Not getting attention sometimes can be hard, but fighting for it will hurt you even more in the long run. My advice for this chapter is that you need to find your own 'why', and if your 'why' is to impress somebody, or to get attention, or to only do it for money, try to dig deeper and try to find out what else is inside of you. If there is something else which is your unique 'why', concentrate on the other part of your 'why' it will make you happier. Some people on this planet don't want to give you attention, and you are not the person to change that. It is the person himself, who needs to change it.

You might ask yourself what now is your 'why'?

The smooth and clear answer about my unique 'why' is that I want for myself to make a good impact on this world. I want to help people grow and help people who need help to find to themselves. I want people to feel stronger, show them how to love, and most importantly help them to love themselves, which is the essential attribute every person needs to have. Additionally, I also want to build up a brand which helps the environment, improve the societal issues and make the world a better place, and why? Because it is my purpose in this world!

Chapter 3
Self-love and appreciation for a more fulfilled life!

"Encourage yourself, believe in yourself, and love yourself. Never doubt who you are."

Stephanie Lahart

This chapter is all about yourself; we will talk about your purpose in this world and the reason why you are here. One of the most essential part of it is, of course, the self-love. The quotation of Stephanie Lahart, an entrepreneur and writer, should be the best example and belief sentence which you shouldn't forget while reading this chapter. It reflects the truth, you should be your most prominent love in life, and while loving yourself, success will get easier.

However, how will YOU be able to love yourself? Not doubting about your strengths and realising that you can achieve everything?

It starts with forgiveness.

Yes, you read correctly. Forgiveness is the key to self-love. It is the step you need to take to be able to live your full potential. Forgive yourself first about everything you feel wrong of. Maybe it is lying, like boasting about success, which you did not achieve in reality to seek temporary attention, cheating, bullying, or stealing, whatever it is, forgive yourself for your doings. By forgiving yourself, you also start to build an emotional relationship with your victims, which will even help you more to forgive, as the victims will realise and feel your forgiveness towards them. Everything happens for a reason, and what happens is not forgettable, but it is forgivable. Also, start to forgive the people who did not do good to you. These people also made it for a reason or out of emotion. Try to look from the view of the people whose doings were harmful to you and try to imagine what their reason for their doing is or was. Write down whom you would like to forgive for, your doings, as well as the doings where you were a victim. Mostly we are carrying around this weight on our shoulders, and do not realise how much it is holding us back in living our best potential, and it is the burden for self-love. We are angry or disappointed in our doings, which keeps us back from loving our self, or other people doings hold us back of loving our self, as we think we are not good enough or loveable.

Furthermore, holding on to the past often hurts a lot and can affect our body and mind. If you believe it or not, holding on to negative experiences affects our immune system, which results in being weaker, sick, and in the end, it will tear you down. Try to let go by forgiving these people.

Later on, you can think about your environment. What kind of situation are you in? Who are the people that surround you every day? What are these people doing to you, and most importantly, do they bring you any further in your life and your goals?

If your answer is no, you might think about changing your environment. I can tell you a story of my personal life. As I have mentioned before, I had time in my life where I was drinking much alcohol. My friends and I were partying every weekend from Friday to Sunday, and often I did not even come home on the weekend because I went from party to party. This might not seem like a big problem, as I was a teenager and enjoyed my time, but the fact that we drank a lot also let me do many things which I regret now. Often, I was unfair to other people or embarrassed myself. Some of my friends even ended up doing drugs because alcohol wasn't enough anymore. Thank god, I decided to change my life before that happened. I stepped back, concentrated on more important things than partying, and started to change my life. A lot of these friends still have the same situation, their only purpose is getting wasted on the weekend, and already on Monday hope that it will be Friday soon. These people did not give me what I wanted in life, and changing my life was the best decision

I have ever made so far. I found new friends very soon. Of course, also there, partying is a big part of the life, as we are young and we want to have fun, but I am also able to talk to my friends about life, about the future, about their and my goals. It is incredible how my life changed since I took the decision of changing my environment.

Quickly write down what your environment is about, who are the people you are with, and how are they helping you to get to your goal? These can be friends, family, or relatives. You will probably realise that there are people who are not helping you in any way of getting where you would like to be. It is your decision what you will do with these connections, but as my experiences told me, it is best to try and avoid the environment which is not bringing you any further. The step of saying "No, I want to change my life" takes much courage, and you might feel a little lonely after you make your decision. You might also feel worthless without your friends, and you might also experience that people talk about you and your choice behind your back. This single time is the best to figure out what you want. Do not directly get to know new people and also do not directly get into new relationships. Enjoy the time alone and decide for yourself who and what you will get into your life. As soon as you have figured out what you want, you will go through a significant process, probably the biggest in your life, because you are on your way towards living your full potential! You will grow, and you will make come true what you have always dreamed of! It would help if you had people in your life who do support you, who are there with you in your bad times, but these people should also support what you want, not what they want you to do. Proving your success to the people who have never believed in you, is an indescribable feeling, and trust me, if you are starting by selecting your environment, you will be there very soon!

Other than looking at your environment, you should have a look at your activities. What is your day to day life? What is your job? How is the family doing, and what are you investing your time in?

I often heard people telling me how busy they are and how they do not have any time doing what they want. They do not have free time and run from appointment to appointment. When I ask them what they are doing that makes them so busy, they most of the time do not even know. Since we humans have existed, stress has always been part of our life. Stress is nothing terrible, and humans are even striving to be stressed. Due to the epinephrine released when we are stressed, we feel worthy, and we feel like we are doing something. If you believe it or not, we are striving for stress but unfortunately, with unnecessary things. Often, we get stressed or busy with things which do not bring us to where we want to be, and while doing things which do not help us bring us one step further towards our goal, we feel empty. If you want to love yourself, start investing your time in things which do bring you nearer to your final goal, and you will realise that you and your life are loveable.

We already know, that self-love in general is crucial to have, but even harder to learn, which applies to all age groups, genders, religions, and humans living on the planet. Self-love is a topic people do not want to talk about that often because, inside the heart of every individual, we know, how hard it is, to accept and to love the human being you are. However, nowadays it is even harder.

A long time ago, children grew up without any technology and no judgments of people they didn't even know. People grew up in a way that they were having friends, family, and relatives, but didn't care that much about other people, their life or problems. This changed dramatically during the last 20 years. We all know that technology grew rapidly from the late nineteenth century and that more and more external influences entered our life. Of course, self-love was already an issue before this time. Children also got bullied, because of their social status, weight or similarities, but the way children grow up nowadays in on another level.

Children nowadays grow up with technology, social media, online games, and more. I know children who are ten years younger than me who have a newer iPhone than myself. I know parents who give their kids a movie when they want to have time for themselves. I know kids who are using technology to bully, and I know what kind of effect this has on the whole environment of every young individual. When I grew up, I also had a phone quite early, it was a Motorola, which you needed to slide up to open. I mainly had it for emergencies and to be in contact with my mother, as my way to school was pretty long. Even at this young age, we all had phones, which are not comparable anymore with the phones you buy nowadays, but the bullying already started by comparing the phones by each other. We could barely use them but already started to let other people feel bad about the brand, functionality, and age of the phones they had. This, of course, got way worse today. By the evolving social media, which more and more kids join, the extension it has reached is unbelievable. Kids get bullied online in worldwide applications like Facebook, open to the whole world to see what is happening, and nobody can do anything against it. This is not only happening with young children, but also with people my age. How many times did you already see racist or anti LGBT comments on Facebook?

These comments, posts, and open-ended ways of discrimination are one of the reasons why most of us are not able to love ourselves. We see these things online and start asking ourselves if our way of thinking, acting and living is right. We start doubting about ourselves and stop to love us, the way we are. We stop to love ourselves, and this is the moment where we fall into depression. It is like a closed door, which is separating us from our real purpose in life, separating us from success and most importantly separating us from living a happy and fulfilled life. However, do you know what is sometimes most important in life? To give a sh*t. Sometimes it is essential to not care what other people think about you. Other than that, it is proven that most of the people who bully others are jealous about the life the person is living.

Always remember that the people who want to bring you down are down and that these people are very jealous about what you are doing in life. Maybe you are gay and are outing yourself on Facebook. People will start talking, but deep inside of them, they are just jealous about your braveness. Maybe you started to work at a new, higher position in a company and you are posting it online; people will also start talking and perhaps commenting it in a way that you do not earn to have this position. Deep inside of them, they are jealous, and maybe also would like to have this position, and grow their career. Perhaps it is even your family, which is treating you jealously, they are jealous!

The second reason why it is so hard for us to love ourselves is social media as a contact where we can get attention. I am sure that people who read this book are also counting their likes on Instagram, and I am also sure that there are people who are faking their lifestyle on social media, to look better. Again, it is proven that there are people who are doing these things, just to get positive attention for themselves. This attention maybe cannot be found outside in real life, and that's why more and more people change towards this behaviour. We give so much attention to other people's opinions that we forget to consider our own opinion. For us and this generation, it is so important to have a good reputation for everyone and to be flawless. By always being as the other people would like us to be, we forget to be ourselves, to live our life. Please do me a favour and start with small steps to care less and less about what other people think about you. If you want to live your purpose, what you only can achieve by loving yourself, you need to live the life you want and not the life other people want you to live. Social media is good. I am not saying you should delete all of your accounts; I am saying that you should understand what social media does to you, and to then take your outcomes, to build your self-love, without considering any other opinion.

It is your life, live it!

Chapter 4
The Purpose

*"The person without a purpose is like
a ship without a rudder."*

Thomas Carlyle

Welcome to the chapter which will bring you much further in what you want to achieve. The following pages are all about finding your purpose to achieve what you want. Even in the seventeenth century, humans already knew how essential a purpose in life is, like Mr Thomas Carlyle, the British historian quoted. However, what is the purpose of each individual, and how are we supposed to find it?

Before I tell you how to find your purpose, I first want to state some facts to make this chapter a little more practical.

You should know that every person on this planet has an individual purpose. You should know that no one has an purpose that is by any means better or worse than another. The particular purpose is something you are born with, and our challenge on this world is to figure out what it is. Our aim is not a problem we need to solve, and we also do not need to search for it. The purpose is a destiny, which is inside our heart, and it is just waiting for the right time to get discovered. You also do not need to think about what your purpose could be, and most importantly, you never should set up a purpose which you might feel could fit you. The goal needs to be discovered, without any external influences who tell you what your purpose is. Of course, it sometimes helps to get external feedback on what your goal could be, but in the end, you are the person who needs to find out what your real destiny in this world is. The purpose in life is also not applicable to only one spectrum in life, like your job. It is applicable on your whole life; this includes, your family, friends, hobbies or way of living.

I hope this helps you a little to realise how certain it is to find out what your purpose is if you are seeking a better life. I also want to tell you that there is no problem in not knowing what your purpose is, and for what reason you are on this earth. It is something we all need to figure out, and I will help you get nearer to your unique purpose. Don't stress about what your purpose could be, and do not concentrate too much on finding it, because it will find you, and will guide you to where you are destined to be. Maybe you also already know what your destiny in this world is, but be aware, that the following words might change your understanding of your purpose or perhaps also show you even more apparent, that you are on the right way.

Let's start with some examples, which might help you understand even better that it takes time to figure out your purpose. There are many examples on the internet mainly of celebrities like the Rock Johnson and his $7 moment. I want to tell you a story you might not know until now. The story is not about a celebrity and not about somebody famous; it is about my lovely mum.

She grew up in a hectic environment. Her dad had a restaurant and was always working together with his wife on serving the guests, preparing the meals and cleaning the restaurant. My mum also needed to help from a very early age in entertaining the guests and telling them jokes, to order another round of beer at the bar. After several years she decided to move out from her home, she was only 15 years old but couldn't stand her stepfather anymore, with whom she lived after her parents got divorced. She wanted to finish her high school diploma but didn't have money for living. At the end of the month, she didn't even have enough money to cook a meal and finally decided that she would not be able to finish school due to the financial problems. Afterward, she started working in at a dentist's office but pretty fast realised, that is not what she wanted to do. The problem was that she didn't know what her purpose was at the time. Afterward, she started working at the bank and worked all her way up to be the bank manager of a small department in Germany. However, even this job wasn't her destiny in this world. She quit and got to know my father. My mum helped him to grow on the success ladder until I was born. At this time, my father was working in Nigeria for a logistics company. I was only six weeks old when I also came to Nigeria to live there. My mum told me that the time there was very hard and that we needed to flee after there was war in the city, we were at the time residing in. However, after my parents and I came back to Switzerland, my dad didn't want my mum to work, but rather to look after me. Pretty soon, my mum realised that this is not her purpose in life. She developed this massive strive after doing what she wanted to do. After all she went through in her childhood and teenage life; she finally wanted to achieve her destiny. Her destiny to help other people!

She built up a small company in Switzerland, by giving massages and yoga lessons, but then my father and my mother got divorced. But not even a divorce could get her down to quitting what she loved to do. Two years later, my dad claimed the house we were living in, and my mum decided to move into a big house, with a vast garden together with her brother and sister in Germany. The home is lovely, all surrounded by nature and peace, but the problem was nobody knew my mother at this time. If you believe it or not, she again did it. She again built up her empire, which is giving endless yoga lessons, earning different awards, and is helping people in relationships and addictions, and still earning the respect she is destined to get.

This story hopefully shows you how important it is to find your purpose in life, how important it is, to try different ways, until finding your destiny, and how important it is to trust yourself on the journey of finding your purpose. Often people also find their purpose in their private life with the family; it is possible that your mission is to be an amazing mum to your kids or being a lovely husband or wife, everybody has a different purpose in this world. To find out what your real goal is, you also might ask yourself, am I doing what I like to do? Is the way I am going right now only an experience, or is it my destiny? Is the purpose you might already have found your real purpose? Honestly, I didn't find my purpose, either. I am experimenting with my life, I am trying different ways, and eventually I will find my goal with time. This story should also show you that it doesn't matter what kind of environment you grew up or are living in right now. The past is unchangeable, but the future is what we can form for ourselves.

As a piece of small advice on how it might be easier for you to find your purpose, you should give everything you can in each moment of your life. Try always to give your best and try to always give all your emotions into what you are doing right now. By feeling what kind of emotions come back from your current activity, you will soon realise what you want. If what you are doing right now, is not giving you positive and abundant emotions back, try to change the track you are on right now and try something else. Everybody will get to the point where they realise what they really want. Some people will find it early and some people later, but we all will know it one day. After you have found your purpose, and you feel the positive emotions you get back from your activity, I promise you, that success in what you are doing will come way easier. You will feel at the time, how your activity will fill up your heart with happiness and abundance, and that is the moment you know, what your purpose in this world is.

We all are, in general, very purpose-driven. We all want to have a life full of meaning and want to enjoy every second of our life while doing what we like. The thought about a purposeful life is, unfortunately, most of the time not enough. We often find purpose in our private life and are very much connected to the whole world due to technology. We most of the time have a friend's base, where we like to meet up, connect and network, but still, most of us, do not feel like we have found our real purpose. Most of the time, the problem lies in our job. We graduate from school, and the whole world is open to us. Maybe we go studying or start working in a company which initially is interesting for us. We begin to learn and also enjoy the first few months at our new working place, but then something unexpected happens.

It is proven by so many scientists that we are searching for purpose and want to make a real impact in our life. As already discussed in the chapter before, our parents tell us throughout our whole childhood that it is possible to achieve whatever we want and that we can make an impact on this world. By stepping into reality, we again realise how hard it is to make an impact on this world and how much work it requires. To come back to the job situation, we are very soon depressed. We realise that it is way harder to make an impact in comparison to what people told us. Especially in a big company where thousands of people are working. The traditional jobs we have are minimal jobs, and most of the time when we start working, we enter a completely new industry. Maybe you are an assistant or even a manager, but the real thought behind making an impact is way too hard to realise. Yes, we are very impatient. Again, this is not necessarily our fault, because when we look into our childhood and teenage time, you will realise that everything you wanted came instantly. You want to watch a movie; go to Netflix. You want to have something; your parents buy it. You want to travel; buy an airplane ticket for the same day. Everything we want in our life, everything we are striving for was instantly happening to us. However, in reality, and especially into the attention of making an impact, life is different. It takes time, and it takes hard work to change something in this world or to make an impact. Precisely these two things, make us quit. The thought about actually working for something, not having it instantly, investing time and dedication. To repeat it clearly, this is something we need to learn. You as an individual probably have never learned anything like this throughout your life, but it's time to follow your path. I can advise you to use the information in this chapter to build up your purpose, to find your purpose and to learn not to quit, not to run away because you are afraid, but to stand your whole strength and work on your life purpose. To take small steps at a time, but continuously work on your goal, which helped me, to overcome this fear of actually investing time and energy into my purpose.

I know that these steps are very hard, especially nowadays, and this is also proven by several scientists, who invested much time to find out more about humans, but I am certainly convinced that everybody can find a purpose in life, which will make you, your life and your future abundant.

I believe in you and your purpose, and I certainly know that you can reach it when you follow the words you just read!

Chapter 5
Dream it!

"Dream the impossible. See the invisible. Pursue the intangible. Achieve the incredible."

Matshona Dhliwayo

Congratulations, you arrived in Chapter 5, where we will talk about your dreams. This chapter and the following words will show you how certain it is to dream, to dream big and to have meaningful goals. I will show you that if you dream hard and big enough, you can achieve whatever you want in your life. The past chapters helped you to get prepared for this one. You know what you want in life, you know how to love yourself, and most importantly you know how to figure out what your real destiny and purpose are in this world. All of these attributes are important to dream big, to think about what your life will be, and to dream about what you want to achieve in your life. All of these attributes can again be used in all of your life; it does not mean you only achieve something in your job and dream about your next promotion. You can dream about how your future life will be, how you will live, how your family will look like, what your social environment will be like, and much more.

I encourage you to dream big, big dreams attract big personalities, and precisely this is what we are striving for. We are striving for growth in our whole life; our brain is programmed to learn, to grow, and most importantly, to dream. So, open up to your dreams, your thoughts, and your feelings.

When I first worked at a company based in Zurich, Switzerland, I had colleagues who have worked in this same company for decades. Every morning they stepped in, and in the evening they stepped out, decades without any happiness, dreams or opportunities. They just stepped in and stepped out. Not one day I saw them smiling or enjoying what they were doing; they just did what they were supposed to do, not more, and not less. For the company, of course, these employees are great. They had the experience they needed, and they always finished their job at the same level of excellence, but what about the employee? Do you think there is any space for dreaming? Any space to strive for a better life? The answer is no.

You might be stuck in the same situation, maybe it is a job or a relationship, or perhaps it is the family. We often get stuck in circumstances, which take away the inner desire of ourselves to dream.

Maybe your dreams even got buried already, from past mistakes, discouragement, breakups or divorces or perhaps even low self-esteem, however, we have the potential of greatness inside of us, inside of our heart and soul. You might doubt and fall back into your old state of mind, which takes you away from your dream. You might not understand what you did wrong, why a marriage or a relationship did not work out, or why your job wasn't as good as expected. Your dreams might get buried in the endless cycle of depression of not being able to dream, of being stuck in the same situation. Precisely that is why it is yours and everybody else's time to stand up again, to dream again and to strive for what you want. Even if you have setbacks, things are not working out the way you want them to; our dreams are still alive. They are still visible deep in the inside of us, and it is our responsibility to let them awaken.

As a small example from my own life, I can tell you how much I was stuck in my life, how I forgot to dream and thought I would never be able to dream big and live the dream. As I told you before I was with my friends, we didn't do anything which might help us in our future, which might let us achieve the goals and dreams we have. I was in a relationship, which clearly showed me that with this partner at my side, I would never be able to dream big, to achieve my big dreams. I was living in a small village with big dreams, and my partner always told me that for her, there was no life outside of this village possible. Getting a job and working for the next 40 years, growing a small family and paying bills was her understanding of life. I had a completely different understanding of life, wanted to get out of this village, see the world, live abroad, and achieve my dreams. It held me back from my dreams, and for a short time I even thought my understanding of life might be wrong. I want to thank god and especially my mother for showing me that my understanding was a different one, that my understanding is my destiny, part of my purpose, and that nothing should hold me back from going my own, unique way. Here I am, living in London and studying what I always have dreamed of.

Before I started working in Switzerland, I went to school like every other student in my age. I worked so hard to get good grades to make myself and my family proud. I tried to search for motivation, but I just couldn't find it. My grades got worse day by day, I started cheating in my exams, to at least make my family proud, but deep inside of me I knew it was wrong, I knew that the school I studied at couldn't give me what I wanted, and that it was not teaching me things which motivate me. It can't give me knowledge which will bring me further in my life. I decided to start working in Switzerland, first in a pharmaceutical company, and yes, finally I found the motivation. I was traveling a lot, took part in important meetings and at only 19 years of age, I managed to work as consultant for another company based in Switzerland. I was so proud during that time, and I finally achieved what I wanted. When I started studying in London, I felt that what I was learning is interesting, and it is helping me towards my destiny. I want to show you; "It is important to dream big."

Through the big dreams we dream, our brain and our full concentration and focus, is only on this one dream we want to achieve, but remember a dream can only become a reality with a goal, a goal you are working for. By having your vision and your next goal clear in your mind, heart, and soul, success will flow way easier, and you will achieve your dreams faster. Also, make sure that nobody can talk you out of your dreams. Often family or friends are the ones who say, "You are dreaming too big," "You will never be able to achieve this." Do not forget that those people are either jealous or they are afraid of you making mistakes. Let them talk and think that you will not be able to be successful in every area of your life until you show them. Believe me; it is an indescribable feeling showing your doubters, how successful you are. Try to take people with you, who believe in you, and also try to convince your doubters about your dreams and goals. You will need people who follow you. Those who genuinely believe in what you are doing are the ones who will help you achieve your goal, remember, we do not need to go this path alone. Tell your mind and your brain that "Dreams will come true" and that "Everything is possible." If your mind, heart, and soul are entirely concentrated on achieving your dream and goal, you will be able to get there, everybody can! There is a known quotation, which is describing this very good, "Everybody is hungry, but only a few are willing to hunt." Be the person who hunts after your dreams, be the person who believes in your dreams and give everything you need to achieve your goals!

Chapter 6
The Power of your Mind

*"Change your mind,
change your life"*

Amadeus Lombardi

This chapter will explain to you more deeply, what kind of impact thoughts have on your life. It is essential to understand that our thoughts and our mind are bringing us where we want to be. This might seem illogical to you, but I ensure you that positive thoughts will help you immensely, to live a happier life.

How many times per day would you say that you have thoughts, consciously or unconsciously, what do you think is the number?

When I first asked this question to some of my friends, their answers were hilarious. Some of them said 100, or 1000. One friend even said 10,000, but do you want to know what the correct answer is?

Several scientists, studies and writers already

confirmed that we have between 12,000 to 60,000 thoughts a day! This is incredible, isn't it? The average of this number is 36,000 thoughts a day, so if we take an average person, this person has about one thought every 2.4 seconds. Imagine how hard our brain is working every day to think, to make assumptions, and to help us to understand different things in different ways.

If I would ask you now, how many of these thoughts are positive and how many negative, you would probably answer, that you have more positive thoughts then negative ones. It is reasonable to assume that the positive thoughts overrule the negative ones, but what do you think?

Go deeply in your heart, try to remember some of the thoughts you had today, doesn't matter if positive or not, and try to figure out how many there are on every side. Whatever your answer is, it is probably wrong.

According to "Faith, Hope and Psychology", an online blog by Stephen Galloza, about 80% of our thoughts are negative. This means that about 29,000 of these daily thoughts of an average person are negative. So many negative feelings on one day, isn't that crazy?

If my calculations are correct, we spend every day 19.2 hours on negative thoughts; thoughts which are not bringing us further in our life, thoughts that are keeping us back from living our potential or taking the next step towards our success. If an average person has this many negative thoughts a day, I don't want to know what a person with 60,000 thoughts a day will think about.

This is the answer to the negativity inside all of us. Our life is all about this. You probably already heard that we are all striving for a happier life, quality over quantity, and these kinds of things. That's at least what some people found out. However, as I have started investigating more time into the fact that we have so many negative thoughts, it just got so much clearer to me, than never before; let me explain what I mean.

Nowadays, we have the highest rate of physical illnesses around the world. One of the highest suicide quotes since the Vietnam War and moreover, more and more people falling into depression, but why?

In the beginning, it was hard for me to understand why people are striving for a better life, knowing that these rates I just showed you are increasing day by day. How can it be that we want to have a more fulfilled life, but do not manage to get there?

My personal answer to this is the media. I already gave you my point of view towards technical devices and social media, but would also like to talk about the media, and how it is manipulating each and every one of us. Since I am living in London, I have never been able to see the news on the TV, which I used to watch back home, simply because I do not have a TV. Therefore, I sometimes go onto my phone to check the news or read the left behind newspaper in the tube. Whenever I open up the news, I always see the negativity about everything. "Somebody got killed on London streets," "There are more and more homeless people," "more and more people can't afford a living anymore" and so on. It is an endless story of negativity. Guess what, the London newspaper *The Sun* has about 33 million readers every month; 33 million people who are reading this negativity. It is not the fault of the newspaper; it is the readers' fault.

As several studies showed, we humans love drama. If we don't have drama with somebody in our life, we watch a TV show or Facebook videos, where drama is displayed. It is kind of entertaining for us, something we can think about and something which gives us the ability to talk to others about a specific event. Every newspaper and also movie, as well as marketing specialists, use this habit for their own success. Wouldn't we be bored to read stories that the world famous Great Barrier reef in Australia is finally not anymore on the threatened world heritage list, or that the oceans get cleaner and cleaner every day by thousands of people who get our garbage out of it? Alternatively, the deforesting in the Amazons area gets less and less due to the brave organisations who hold against it? I think that this is not boring at all. I think these are precisely the news stories we need, to get inspired and to be positive about our lives.

If you would read these kinds of stories every day, or even if you would concentrate on successes, rather than failure, do you not think that your life would be more positive?

I am positively sure it would be. Try it out, and you will see the difference.

Secondly, I want to talk about our mind, which is, of course, influenced by our thoughts. At the beginning of this chapter, I told you that a positive mind could bring you wherever you want to be, and that's true.

Imagine if all of your thoughts were positive; think about how your life would change. Would you be more motivated, would be more efficient? Would you be happier?

I think these are questions we have all already asked ourselves, if not please take a few minutes and think about them.

It is improbable that this is how your life will be at one point, as there are always things we need to solve, or problems which arise on our way towards success, however, it is possible to make our lives more positive and fulfilled.

Often, I hear other people say, "It will either way not work," "Why should anybody buy my product or service?" "I am not good enough." I am sure also you already had thoughts like this and have invested time into something which didn't go according to your plan. I can assure you if you think in the same way like these examples I gave to you, you will not achieve your goals, find your purpose, or have any success, in what you are doing.

Why? Because you train your mind to be negative.

Some of my former classmates often said, "I will never get an A," "This is just too hard for me," and believe it or not, it is. These people often didn't get their A's, ended up with a lousy grade and they got even more depressed than before. It is true; a positive mind gives you a positive life. When I was going to school, I thought like this. My thoughts were negative, like; "I am not interested, this is not helping me, I don't want to do this, I either way will get a bad grade," and it happened. I was unmotivated, tired, and finally ended up with the bad grade, which I trained my mind to get. Since I have got out of school, I tried more and more to change my way of thinking, for example, with the first job I had. I always told myself that I am great that this company waited for someone like me and that I would be able to make a difference. Even if some of these things aren't true, I ended up having a great time, I travelled around the globe and got to know new people, and I even think that I was able to make a difference in one or another way.

To conclude, it is essential for you, to change your way of thinking dramatically, stay away from the negative media, which confronts each of us day by day and try to see in everything that is coming into your life the positive aspect. Try to change your mind positively, believe in yourself and the power you have, and like everything else, love yourself for who you are!

Chapter 7
The influence of Technology

*"Life is about feelings
rather than showings."*

Amadeus Lombardi

Throughout this book, we talked a lot about the influence technology has on us, and especially on the younger generations out there. Of course, technology is not bad, and we all can be delighted that it is in our life. We all know, that technology is helping us a lot in our day to day life, and how we can take benefit of it. However, in this chapter, I will also explain how technology and especially social media is changing our lives negatively.

The quote is showing the first and essential aspect of social media. As you know and probably already heard several times, social media is excellent for swallowing feelings.

Yes, most of us only post positive things about our lives. Every social media account is looking very positive, and only the good things are showing, which is a human instinct. We want people to think how great our life is, how we do not have any problems, and how often we go traveling, what we can buy and what we can afford.

Often life looks different; often we have negative feelings, maybe not everything in our life is as high as it seems like on our online accounts. Often, we hide the negativity and feel like a better person if we can post only positive things. Usually, we try to impress people, who do not even care, but it lets us feel better in our skin, which is again connectable to our self-love. As most people are not any celebrities, who get a lot of attention from outside, we at least try to get positive feedback online. We are happy when somebody is complimenting us, even if it might be fake. It lets us feel better. However, let's dig deeper into what is influencing this behaviour.

Fact is, we love having attention; that's why it is so important to give much attention to babies and small children. A baby could die by not receiving enough attention and skin contact, which is scientifically proven. As we grow up, of course, we might not get as much attention as we got when we were younger. We are not anymore, the small 'cutie pie', but rather the grownup, who is not allowed to show any feelings in public, that's at least what we think. We are not the small kid anymore, which always gets attention when it starts crying, but we should instead stop crying in public, as it might be embarrassing, which is a human way of thinking;

the way most of us got taught and a social standard, which gets outlived on this world. However, even when we grow up, we have feelings which we might want to share with the world. It is an ability we need to learn in the process of growing up, to get stronger, to not necessarily show our emotions whenever we feel like, to not start crying whenever we want something, or did you ever see a 17-year-old boy crying when he didn't get a new phone? I didn't. However, in the social standard nowadays, you might have already seen that a three-year-old girl started crying and the parents didn't make any effort to give the kid attention, other than just giving the kid a phone with the newest Barbie series playing. The kid stopped crying and watched the series. Is that not crazy? Do you not think that this influence is negative on a child? Do you not believe that these experiences will influence the kids' behaviour?

I am 100 % sure that these ways are influencing children and their process of growing up. I often see 9- to 11-year-old kids, who have a newer iPhone than me, they play games on their phone, and there is no social interaction at all, which is the next step of the process of growing up. Go to an elementary school nowadays. Kids play games on their device, it is entirely silent, and they are only concentrating on the technology they are using. Ten years ago, when I went to school, we played soccer, screamed, ran, played games, or talked to our classmates, which has completely changed over the years. The negative consequence of this is that kids do not learn at all to have any social interaction with other people. They are only concentrating on the virtual world they are living in, and think that the people whom they get in contact with online are their new friends, people they never met in their life.

When Facebook started and invented the friend list, people started comparing their amount of Facebook friends with other people amount of Facebook friends. Whoever has more, wins. It is crazy, how the word 'friend' changed over the last few years. I can tell you that humans between 15 and 30, who grew up with the technological advancements, do not have the same friends people had 20 years ago. The understanding of friends changed utterly. People nowadays are defining friends as a group of people they spend time with, have an excellent time, go out for drinks, but they could and would never rely on their so-called friends. Is that not crazy? To explain once more what I mean by that, I need to go back in time for about 30 years. My mom once told me that whenever she was on skiing holidays with her family, which took part every winter between Christmas and New Year, they didn't have phones. It, of course, happened, that she and the rest of the family had different plans, which meant that they agreed on a time, they would meet in a restaurant, or at the hotel again. It always worked out. She also told me, that when she went to school, she agreed on a time with her friends to meet on the playing ground after school, and without any telephone, or contact, at the agreed time, everybody met at the playing field.

Nowadays, we have phones, where we are in contact with other people all the time, and kind of this way of just agreeing on when you will meet with your friends or family does not work out anymore. How many times did you already reassured yourself with your friends on when you are meeting? How many times was there already a miscommunication? How many times, did you already wait for friends because they forgot or had something better to do? It is true, we cannot rely on our friends anymore, even if we have the possibility of being in contact with them 24/7. The situation of not trusting and not building on our friends anymore means that our self-esteem, the self-love, the love and support we would feel from our friends is not there. We do not just call our friends anymore when we feel down, or if we have a feeling, we want to discuss with them, but we turn to social media.

Scientists found out that social media and the attention we are getting from there releases a chemical, the so-called dopamine. This chemical lets us feel good, it gives us the feeling of getting attention, and it makes us feel released and unusual, which is precisely the chemical we as a generation need. As I have already discussed earlier, our parents are always telling us how great we are, how we can achieve everything, but as soon as we get released into real life we experience that not everything is possible, and that you cannot have everything instantly as you want it. Therefore, we are turning to social media, which is releasing dopamine which lets us feel good. Dopamine is also the chemical which gets released when we drink or take drugs, it allows us to feel suitable for a short moment, or one night, before we again fall into depression. Dopamine is also the reason why we feel good when we get likes on Instagram or get attention for our WhatsApp message.

Imagine life as a straight line. Sometimes, we have a good day, sometimes a bad day, and therefore the line goes up or down. If we now drink or take drugs, the line goes up as we feel free and released. After the night out the line goes down again, as we realise that this was only a feeling and not our real life. That's why we go back to alcohol and drugs and that is how addictions evolve. Fortunately, all around the world, we have age restrictions for alcohol, and most countries even forbid drugs by law. The question is now; why is there no age restriction on social media?

You might say, that Facebook has age restrictions, but let's be honest, most of us have faked their age, to get access to the platform.

Did it work? Yes, it did.

Dopamine is the reason we post positive pictures,

why some of us show off online to get attention, and the reason why we instead turn back to our phones rather than to have face to face discussions with our friends. The most important fact now is to understand that addictions most likely get discovered by an individual during the time of growing up. Most addicted people get addicted to their young age and then carry it around for the rest of their life if they don't take any action against it.

The question is: what does this have to do with social media?

The problem lies in the timing. When we are kids, we want to have the attention of our parents, we want our parents to be proud of us, but as we go through our teenage time we understand and realise that we also wish to the attention of our friends, of people in our life, who are related to us. That's precisely the reason why we often are pissed about our parents, pissed about what they want to tell us, and suddenly turn our backs on them. As I have mentioned earlier, most young adults commit that they cannot rely on their friends, that they might leave them if they find anything better than them, and therefore we turn towards virtual friendships, which we find online.

Yes, we are happy when somebody is confirming our friend request, and when our Instagram picture has five more likes than the previous one, which unfortunately leads to an addiction, an addiction which already young teenagers have, and a habit which can ruin your life, cost a lot of money and let you feel bad over time.

This social media addiction is also the reason why we always need to have it with us. We always carry around a device, where we can use social media, which leads to the problem of not having any social interaction anymore. When you wait for somebody in a restaurant, you are most likely turning to your device, if you are on holidays at the beach for relaxing, you are most likely turning to Facebook. It is an addiction which we need to understand is taking away the joy in our life. Maybe you have also already experienced a situation where you see something you have never seen before in your life, like dolphins in open waters jumping around the boat you are on. I experienced precisely the same situation about one year ago when I was on holidays. I went on a trip with the boat, and lucky me, I saw dolphins jumping in front of the ship. Everybody instantly got out their mobile phones, cameras, iPads, whatever they had with them to take a photo. Until some of the people even managed to turn on the camera, the dolphins were gone. I am not saying that it is terrible taking pictures, but in this situation I could see the frustration in these people's faces. They neither managed to take a photo, nor did they enjoy the moment of being so near to these fantastic animals. We often lose joy in life, as we always have the need to fix every moment in life forever on a picture.

We lose the ability of just enjoying the moment, a moment which gets set in our brain, a moment we wouldn't forget if we wouldn't be concentrating on our devices or social media, a moment which can be so valuable to us.

Earlier in this book, I talked a little about the fact that we people nowadays get everything instantly. You want something, you can order it, and it will arrive the next day. In fact, Amazon sometimes even does same day delivery. You want to watch a movie, log on to Netflix; you want to find a partner go to Tinder. What I want to say is that everything we want in life gets to us instantly, everything besides real love, happiness, and the impact we want to do on this world. It is hard for our mind and body to understand that these three things will not get into our life instantly, like everything else. Therefore, we often get depressed, we feel like we have no impact on this world, we feel like it is now the third relationship which is not working out, or we feel like we are just not happy with the way we are. It is so crucial to understand that these things take time. It takes time to build up real love. In previous relationships, I made the same mistake. After feeling a little joy and appreciation, I directly went into relationships, precisely because of the reason that we feel alone, that we do not feel like we can trust anybody. Only the smallest kind of appreciation, attention, and commitment leads us to decisions which in the long run hurt us, cost us money and make us feel depressed. Please consider this advice, it can help you so much in the process of finding love, joy, and happiness, and I promise you, if you keep working on it, you will be able to achieve the impact you always wanted to have on this planet.

Chapter 8
How to manage your time?

*"Time is what we want most,
but what we use worst"*

William Penn

As we are slowly approaching the end of this book, I want to give you some more input, of how you will be able to live a better life, a life you are striving for.

Of course, this has a lot to do with managing your time. You probably also experienced days where the time was running. A day where you slept in until noon or didn't accomplish anything until you realise it is already 4pm. These days are vital for us, mainly because our body also needs some rest. Only working, working, working will in the long run not make you happy. You will lose social connections, your body will get weaker, and you won't have time for your family and friends.

The question now is; how can you manage your time in a better way? In a way, that you can take most out of any day, without killing your body or your social ties?

To start, I would like you first to think about how you have invested your time today. What have you done, what are you going to do, what are you doing now? Do you have any external influences, keeping you away of giving 100% attention to this book? Was there anything today which took away your time, something unnecessary?

If you have figured out all of these questions and written them down or just thought about them, you will probably figure out that there are things on your list, which will not help you in any way. For example, if you wrote down, that you were on Facebook this morning for half an hour after waking up or that you had something happening which took away a lot of time and energy, but didn't have any outcome, then you are like 99% of the people living on this planet. I am the same, and it is nothing bad, nothing which will not allow us to live our potential or achieve our goals. The problem behind it is not the time we have spent, but the time we have lost. I already mentioned that everybody has the same amount of time for one day. Everybody has 24 hours or 1440 minutes. Some people invest their time differently, and that is the 1% in this world which will most likely achieve their goals quicker and more efficiently. This is something we need to learn and surely every person can learn it, and I believe that you are on the right way of organising your time in a better way. I will explain to you how.

Imagine you earn £86,400 every day. From Monday to Sunday, every day, there is £86,400 transmitted in your account. Would that not be a great life? In fact, you would do £31,390,000 a year, the life most you, including me, are dreaming of. Of course, you will need to deduct the taxes you are paying on this, the expenditures you have and much more, but for my small example let's take £86,400 as daily income. Of course, you might spend some of this money unnecessarily, just because you can. Of course, you will buy expensive things from high-end brands and expensive cars, you will have a big house and a lot of other things you can afford.

Imagine that you as a person with this kind of income loses £600 a day for something unnecessary; for example, somebody stealing it from you, or you just losing it because it falls out of your pocket. Would you invest the remaining £85,800 to get the lost £600 back? I am pretty sure you wouldn't. However, why? Why would you not spend the rest of your daily money just to get this small sum back? Moreover, why are we making precisely this mistake in our day to day life?

See, every day has 86,400 seconds. So, my story was not really about somebody earning that much money that they could buy a new Ferrari every third day, but about real life. The life you are living.

You have 86,400 seconds every day, and often you lose the rest of your 85,800 by giving all of your time and energy into the ten minutes which didn't work out like you wanted them to do. Every day has bright and dark sides, but are you willing to give up your bright sides, just to think about what is all going wrong?

This is the second time in this book I've told you to not give a sh*t! Your dark sides will be over, and maybe you will lose ten minutes of your day discussing something with your colleague, which is not helping you, or being angry with the person of the call centre who tells you that your contract can't terminate earlier, or maybe you will be even mad about a friend, who is just provoking you because he or she has nothing better to do, this is life.

The first rule of investing your time in a way it makes sense is not to get triggered about things which are not working the way you would like them to. It is essential to give all of your energy towards the positive things; towards the things you are looking forward to. If you fight with your partner, don't just not talk to each other and let it be, this costs way more time and energy than just solving it in the first place. It is also about not overthinking things which didn't work your way, rather than just letting them go.

For the second rule, I would like you to think about your timetable. What is your plan for the day, and have you accomplished it?

What have you been carrying with you for the last half a year?

Did you accomplish everything written on your plan?

If not, you are like 41% of the people living on this planet. Again, this not a significant problem, as you can sort out what you want to do, and what not. First of all, set your priorities. It is one of the most important things, to set priorities and to be aware of where you are going.

What is your ultimate goal, and will all the activities you are investing your time in, help you reach there?

Following this you can find the key to managing your time most effectively; make a plan. Yes, you heard right, a daily plan helps you to organise your time in the right way. However, there is a small problem.

Let's say that in the morning you go for a run, afterwards, shower and breakfast, later on, go to work until 5pm. Then you come home and keep working on the company you want to build up, or are going to spend time with your family. Then you will eat dinner and go to bed. This is a plan most of us have; we don't even need to write it down, as this plan is our daily routine.

As already mentioned, 41% of the people write something on their daily plan but never accomplish it. This means that 41% of the people take their free time, to write out a detailed plan, but will never achieve all of the things written on it, is that not crazy?

I call it dreaming. Dreaming is essential, but without a goal, it will not bring you where you want to be, so what if you would change your daily plan? What if you would make it more detailed and viable for yourself? What if you would only concentrate on the important things, by using your understanding of priorities?

This is exactly the key. Every successful person has a thorough detailed plan for the day. They don't just wake up and lose 30 minutes by scrolling through Instagram; they already, after waking up, make a small step to accomplish their daily plan. Let's say you wake up, and you directly go for a run. This will wake you up and give you energy. After that, you will have breakfast and read the newspaper (the essential parts, not the celebrity drama part). Then you go to work and already while sitting in the tube, train, or bus work on your evolving business. Go to work and have a clear plan of what you are doing. First finish the report, at 10am meeting, afterward answer emails, later go for lunch with XYZ. I think you understand where I want to go; it is about the detailed plan you need to do, and therefore you will not lose any valuable time. Also, make yourself clear, that if you don't finish something in the time you thought you would finish it, plan it again for tomorrow (if not very important or if no deadline). You need to follow your plan and don't give up on it, if you are not able to finish things. In fact, you even learn to manage your time better, as you learn how much time you need for what and how much time you need to plan for the next day for the same task. This is time management.

The third step is to give yourself daily goals. This doesn't only help you to finish things earlier and more effectively; it also rewards you for your hard work. Small goals will motivate you more, give you more energy and finally help you to make your days more time effective and will help you to achieve your goals, even if these are small goals, faster.

Chapter 9
How to live in a
fulfilling relationship?

"True love is about growing as a couple, learning about each other, and never giving up on each other."

unknown

This chapter is all about your relationships. Mainly, I will talk about the relationship between you and your partner, but all of the information can also be transmitted to your friends, your family and your relatives.

To start, ask yourself the question; is your relationship meaningful? Is the love supporting you? Do you have inner thankfulness, to live this relationship?

These questions will show you if your relationship is worthy, if it is meaningful, and if you are actually happy with what you have and with the actual life inside this relationship. I hope that you and your partner can answer these questions with yes, I hope that you answer it honestly, in the way of self-love and self-esteem, and that you don't need to lie and therefore lose your self-esteem. It is essential to understand fully, that the relationship between you and your partner is a gift from heaven; it is a gift you received by God and the endless universe. You should also understand that some gifts are received by the wrong person, just how it is in real life. Some gifts are not supposed to be yours, and some gifts will need to be returned, given away, or some gifts will even break on a heart-breaking way, this is life, this is the life you are living.

To get more into the topic of a meaningful relationship, it is essential for you to understand that the following words are all coming from own experiences, from experiences other people made and some facts are even proven scientifically. To start, I would like you to imagine your dream again. As you have already learned you need to dream big, so what is your dream? Who is in your life? With whom are you sharing your life? What would your dream look like if you would share your life with your current partner (if there is one)? If there is none, who or how will your partner be like?

What does that do to you? Are you feeling happy, emotional, or shocked? How are your heart and soul reacting, if you imagine having your partner in your dream future life? Does it feel good or bad?

From my own experience, I can tell you that sometimes it doesn't feel as good as we would like it to feel. Sometimes, it just doesn't fit, it just doesn't feel right, and that is completely fine. It is nothing to worry about; it is nothing to feel wrong about; it is just a feeling, a feeling coming from your heart. It also doesn't mean that you should quit your relationship or feel like you do not love your partner anymore. It is something you need to work on.

I know this book always tells you that you need to change, that you need to make a change in life or change some of your habits or behaviours. If you do this or not is entirely up to you, it is a recommendation, which will help you for sure, but it is something you need to do, I can't help you with that. However, in my past, I had relationships which didn't work out how I wanted them to work out. In fact, it is not always about what you or I want, it is about what the relationship wants, what both of you want and what is the best for both of your futures. When I still lived at home, in a small village, I had relationships, relationships which first looked very interesting and charming, but with time it turned out that they didn't help me in my future, in my dream and in my purpose, which is none of my ex-partners' faults. As I grew up, I often felt lonely, no father in my life, no significant friendships, and therefore, I decided having a partner could help me love myself. Yes, you might say this is the wrong way to tackle this problem, and you are 100% right, it is. However, some of us, in fact, a lot of us, have the feeling of being lonely, of not making any impact on this world, of not feeling safe and are therefore fleeing into relationships. It is widespread in our life. As we more and more need attention from other people than our parents, it is helping us extremely to get love from somebody whom we think is loving us, in this case, a partner. A partner is giving us attention and love, is telling us beautiful things and is supporting us through our tough times. However, did you ever think about, if your first love, was a person you loved? Was it not a relationship, which gave you the possibility of receiving attention?

In case it was not, I am extremely happy for you, but the truth is that most relationships are based on attention, rather than real love. How does that come about?

As we get released into the real world we realise that life is not as our parents told us it would be. We do not have all the attention on us; we need to share it with other people and cannot just have whatever we want. On the other hand, it, of course, has a lot to do with the fact that we want to learn and experiment, a habit which is inside of all of us.

The problem behind living such a relationship is the love you are not necessarily feeling. It is love, which is not fulfilling you and not making you happy in any way. It is a temporary feeling.

Let's see how you can live a happier relationship and how both partners can get supported inside a relationship.

Traditionally relationships were there to make

kids, to grow the species, and to have somebody on the world with your blood. This perception changed, thank God, and we are giving more and more attention towards the family life. We want to be able to offer our small ones whatever they need, whatever they want. In this case, we need to come back to financial freedom. I promised myself that I would never want to have a kid until I could actually afford to have one until I can show this kid the world, travel to different places, get my kid in contact with other people and cultures and can give back, what I received when I was young. Personally, I think that this is very important. There are a lot of parents out there who need to look after every expenditure, who cannot show their kids the world and even have problems to buy the smallest of things. I am not saying that those people aren't happy, but I am confident that it is harder to maintain such family life. As soon as your kids go to school, they will see what other kids have and then they want the same. I think you know where I want to go with this.

On the other hand, financial freedom can also give you and your partner the possibility to live a happier life. I am not talking about sugar daddies or gold diggers, but about a genuine abundant relationship. When you can afford to buy your girlfriend or wife beautiful jewellery, a cute handbag or invite her for a pleasant holiday on the Maldives, these are things I am talking about. You might think that these gifts are only making you happy for a short time, and yes, that is true, but I am still convinced that money plays a significant role in every person's life.

The next problem is the environment you are living in. Often, I see relationships crumbling because of friends or family; this is a phenomenon, where mainly our parents, or the parents of your partner are afraid of you getting heartbroken. It is essential for you to think about this. Do you feel that your partner could leave you one day, because of somebody else? Could this relationship end in a heart-breaking way? Are you ready for this to happen?

I don't hope that it will happen to you but be prepared for this situation to arise.

Another big problem, which mainly younger people have, is technology.

The previous chapter explained to you already why technology is a problem in our life's nowadays, but let's add in a relationship. It is already hard enough to trust our partner, but with adding on technology, it gets even harder. Let's take social media as an example.

How many of you already checked your boyfriend or girlfriend's phone for suspicious messages? Who previously thought that your partner is writing somebody else online?

You can be pretty sure that this happened or will happen sooner or later. Social media gives us the ability to be in contact with a lot of people. People who can like us, be our ex-girlfriends, or boy-friends, be somebody we met at a party and so on. Please don't understand me wrong, it is essential to keep contact with different people you like, but mainly it is a problem of jealousy, which is hurting or even breaking relationships.

How many times, did you and your partner already have miscommunication over WhatsApp, which ended in a fight or discussion?

Probably a lot. What I am trying to do, and what will also help you, is to concentrate on what you have right now. If I am in a relationship right now, all the external influences shouldn't affect me; I shouldn't give attention to people who are after the relationship. For me, it is a golden rule to stick to what I have. It is also essential to trust your part-ner. By checking his or her phone every day, by being suspicious about his or her doings, the rela-tionship will also suffer immensely under the pres-sure you and your partner go through. However, in case your or your partners feelings would change, it is essential to first finish one thing, before start-ing a new one.

A story states that there was once a man. He had a son and a wife at home but always worked long hours. Every day the work time got longer and longer, but wife and son didn't think anything wrong. "He is probably stressed," "He has proba-bly meetings." In the end, it turned out that this man didn't have meetings, he wasn't stressed, but he had an affair at work with his secretary. This was, of course, a shock for the family, especially because this man came home to his family every evening. Every evening he went to bed with his wife and assured her that everything was okay. One day, like everything, it came out that this man has an affair at work. He could choose between family and affair and chose the family. Everything seemed right again until it started from the beginning. Decide what you want. Don't leave all doors open; otherwise, you will end up on the hallway, as this man did.

Now the question is, how can you be a better lover and bring your relationship to the next level?

There are, of course, a lot of answers to this question. I have collected some from my past experiences about things I think make a relationship abundant. First, you need to understand that relationships traditionally are between man and woman. If this is not the case for you, I can assure you, that most likely one partner in the relationship is the feminine and the other one the masculine part. In fact, we all have masculine and feminine pieces inside of us, doesn't matter about gender. To explain this in a better way, I can give you some examples. We men, like to cuddle, even if this mainly is a feminine part of us. Women also like to tell their opinion, which is very essential in every relationship, which could be understood as a masculine part of them. I think you know what I mean. However, now how can you understand these behaviours and therefore help your relationship?

Men like to get attention, as well as women like the same. If you really love each other, why do you not give each other this attention? It is not about the attention you give or receive inside the relationship; it is also about the outside. Why don't you boast about your partner in public? Like "yesterday he fixed the furniture in our living room. Now it looks so professional, and I am so proud of him." Trust me; it is the small things which make men happy, the appreciation of their work, of the time they invested in making something happen.

For women, it could be; "She played so cutely with the kids we met in the park, and I fell over and over again in love with her." These are things which make our partners happy; it's the small things.

Encourage your partner, show them that you support them through everything, that you are there for them, and push them to give everything they can, to make happen whatever they would like to make happen. Supporting and understanding your partner is one of the most important attributes a relationship should have. Always encourage your partner to go the step, help them to realise that you are there for them, whatever happens.

Share your emotions. It is vital in relationships to talk, to discuss, and to have real communication.

Love and relations are not always about roses and cake; it is about fighting about standing behind your opinion, about showing your feelings. Tell your partner if you don't feel right if something is bothering you. This is the first step to solving it. I am sure that if you tell your partner how you feel, he or she is also able to open up. To talk with your partner about what your heart feels like. Try to solve things with showing emotions and feelings.

Ask your partner for input, for an opinion, and don't be biased about it. Of course, you know that your partner would rather hear something positive, but if you think and feel that he or she is doing something wrong, not good, or not contributing in any way, then tell. Open your mouth, give your input, but be honest, and show your partner that you care.

To conclude this chapter, I would like to talk about you feeling unsupported and unhappy in the relationship you are in. You have now read some information, which can help you to make your relationship get better, but if you feel like nothing is helping any more, it is sometimes better to let go. Once a friend of mine told me "Letting go hurts less than holding on." This sentence helped me to live the life I am living now, it was the point in my life I started to get happy, to work for my purpose and to live my potential truly, maybe it is time for you too.

Chapter 10
The Fear of Failure

"There is only one thing that makes a dream impossible to achieve: the fear of failure."

Paulo Coelho

Do you ever feel like you failed? Would you identify this feeling as a failure? Did you fail because you were fearful of failure, or did you ever think about how failure could benefit you, your future, and your success?

Welcome to Chapter 10, where it is all about failing and the importance behind it. I will explain why it is so important to fail and why we, the people who strive for a more fulfilled life shouldn't be afraid to fail.

You've already learned how to have a vision, how to dream, and you might already see yourself succeeding. This means you are already ten steps ahead of 95% of the people out there in the world. You, your vision, your dreams, and your success make a difference in this world, a difference which we already learned is our unique purpose, your purpose of life.

Let's get started to talk about the topic nobody wants to talk about.

So often I see how people tell you how perfect their life is, how fulfilled they are and that they never failed on their way. I can tell you; this is bullshit. Everybody fails; everybody has the experience of doing something which is not bringing them further in their life. This can be a relationship, a job, or the environment you are living in. It is essential to make these experiences and to learn out of them. When I was in school, I failed. I failed often, and I failed hard. Yes, I did not pass every exam, and yes, I had problems with teachers, which then also ended in a problem with my mother, who just wanted to help me. Yes, I tried different things in my life, and not everything worked out as I have planned it, and yes, it hurt. It hurt my heart, my soul, and my ego. I am sure you also experienced comparable things throughout your life, and I am sure that you also felt the pain of it.

Imagine for a short time, that somebody like Steve Jobs was afraid that people wouldn't like his products or company, would you have an iPhone next to you right now?

These personalities never feared failure. They were so convinced that their invention, their life purpose will change the world and everybody living on it. Your life purpose and you can also change the world. Maybe you are not inventing a new iPhone, but for you and your environment, it is clearly proven that your purpose is making a difference. Perhaps you already experienced this fear. Maybe you even had a great idea or wanted to try to make a difference, but you didn't do it because of this fear. However, imagine how your idea, your passion, and your work could have changed the world.

Just for a short moment, think about what would have changed in your life, how your future would look like if you would have changed, and if you had taken the step to overcome this fear. You need to understand that this shouldn't make you step back; instead it should make you walk two steps forward and face your future.

The importance of failing is described with two main ideas behind it.

If you fail, you learn.

The other idea is to understand that failing is only a starting point of something new, something great. You learn out of failure and can come back stronger, but remember, that only losers stay down after failing and use the negative energy not to get started again. You are not a loser, you are a winner, and you should use this negative energy to do great the next time you are trying. You might fail ten times or 100 times, but you can go back up and start again, and you are going to be stronger, wiser, and more driven every time you fail. See, we shouldn't be afraid to fail; we should love failing. We should be a fan of failing, as much as we are a fan of winning because, without failure, there will be no success.

Another crucial aspect of failing is connecting with a chapter we talked about; it's self-love. It is the key to everything in our life, and without it, we are just floating around without any self-esteem or appreciation for our life and our doings in this world.

Now, to get to the point, I want to tell you how important it is, to accept the nay-sayers, to allow different opinions and different thoughts coming from different people. It is essential to listen to them and to let them get inside of your brain and your heart. What on the other hand side is not okay, is to use these opinions and thoughts against you. Don't let these things impact you on your way, or make you think twice about what you are doing, because this means that you are doubting. You are questioning your vision and your purpose, and precisely this is the thing which will sooner or later lead you to fail.

Once Arnold Schwarzenegger said that he hates 'Plan B' and what he said is so true. As soon as you have a 'Plan B' it is like a safety net for you and your doings. You might even invest more time thinking about 'Plan B' than you are investing in your 'Plan A' which should be the one you should spend your energy on. See, as soon as we start doubting, it is human nature to build this safety net, as soon as we fail, as soon as we make bad experiences, it is normal. Try to overcome this reaction and be 100% convinced that you are doing the right thing and that you are on the right path to achieve it. To be able to think like this about your vision and purpose, you need to love your vision and purpose, and especially you need to love yourself. This also comes with not giving any value to people who might judge you because you failed. By giving these people any value or attention, you are wasting your valuable energy, other than using it for your future, vision, and purpose.

The fear of failure is a big part of our life which holds us back from doing steps into the direction, we would like our life to be. In fact, over 30% of the global population do not get their next steps due to this fear. As already mentioned earlier, our beliefs of being able to achieve everything in life is not necessarily giving us any real motivation. It is instead, giving us more anxiety, as we wouldn't be able to handle the situation of not being able to achieve what we want.

However, what is it really which is giving us this fear? Is it our inside, which holds us back, because we can't handle it?

Of course, there are different ways people will answer this question. As of my own life experiences and understandings so far, I can tell you that there is definitely a fear in us which is holding us back.

I think it is not about the fear of not being able to handle the situation; I believe it is more about the outside world, which is giving us this fear. We already talked about technology in our life, and I think that it is mainly connecting with the fear of showing people we love that we failed. Telling our friends, our family or relatives that the project you were working on, or the company you tried to raise, or the relationship you had didn't work out is the fear which is holding us back. As we more and more are interested in what other people could think about us, our concentration and focus also shapes towards the wrong direction. Yes, I also already invested a lot of energy to try and fit in, to try not to fail, to try and give everything I have to make my family proud, and precisely this was the moment I lost focus on the things which I wanted to achieve, and the things which make me happy. This is not a unique pattern, which only I saw throughout my experiences, but something that several people told me is their reason for not being able to achieve what they wanted to. Earlier, I already told you how important it is to sometimes not care about other people. Even if you try and make your family happy, the most essential and crucial aspect of being successful is to make yourself happy. It would be best if you learned, that failure is part of the success and that there will always be people who will try to keep you down.

New studies are showing that young people are

more open-minded in regard to failure. That these people are more aware of the word failure and how they can use it for their own advantage. In fact, almost 80% of young individuals think that failing might lead them to new ideas and the ability to use it for their benefit. Even if that might be the case, I believe that failure still plays a vital role in our life and future.

However, how will you be able to use success to your advantage, as most young humans respond?

Exactly, it would be best if you came back stronger. It would help if you used your past mistakes to learn from them. You need to understand that whatever doesn't work only helps you to work it out better the next time you are trying, and you need to understand that failure is nothing negative. Something I also already tried is to speak to different people and to try to get them to tell me why they already failed in their life. Fantastic help, for example, was the divorce of my parents. By asking my mum more and more questions, why it happened, and what the problem was, where precisely the marriage failed, I learned how to maintain my own relationship. Of course, I also made mistakes, I also failed, but this is part of the process of learning.

Another example is the kids. When they first learn to walk, they fall again and again, but they always stand up and try again and again. Small kids have this instinct in them to learn, to be like the others, doesn't matter how exhausting hurtful and long it will take, which is a focus and concentration, desire and commitment, we humans, need to learn and maintain. This is the way of failure, and this way is one of the most important ones we need to go through our life.

Are you ready to fail?

Chapter 11
The Power of Success

"Successful people do what unsuccessful people are not willing to do. Don't wish it were easier; wish you were better."

Jim Rohn

Welcome to the most powerful chapter in this book. This chapter is all about SUCCESS! As you already learned, it requires hard work, patience, and constant steps towards your final goal. To start off, I would like to show you the google definition of success; "The accomplishment of an aim or purpose." This shows again how important it is to have a purpose for being able to achieve success, but why?

Imagine you are sitting in a plane, and the pilot has no idea where he is going. Most likely, you will end up at a destination; you didn't like to go or nowhere. You can also project this on your own life.

In this book, I first wanted to help you to find out what you really want, why you want it, to love yourself, to have a purpose, to dream, to understand your mind, how to manage your time, and I wanted to tell you what failure means and now, I am certainly sure, that you are ready to succeed.

What does success mean?

How do you define success, and what do you think is a success for yourself? First, it is essential to know that everybody defines success differently. Being successful can mean that you achieved something big in your job, you found a great working company, you have a great relationship, or that your family life is finally how you would like it to be. Nobody should get judged on their understanding of success, as everybody has a different purpose, which leads them to their inner success, by achieving, and living the purpose. It doesn't really matter, what success really means to you, as the following words are generally speaking about success, in whatever form you are experiencing it.

It is vital to understand that success is not necessarily connected to money and wealth. I am not saying that any wealthy person is not successful, but there is way more you need to take into consideration. If you are willing to earn a lot of money, invest a lot of time and therefore set priorities, which might not make you happy; this means, that you are not successful. Success comes from the inside; it is a feeling you need to have to be able to be successful. It doesn't matter if you are billionaire, founder of any company and you can buy every asset existing in this world. If you do not have any inner freedom, you are not successful. It is proven that only people who are completely happy from the inside are successful. Even if you win tonnes of awards, and everybody is telling you how great you are, this doesn't mean that you are successful. Look at some celebrities, especially musicians, who are famous all around the world. How many need to take drugs, alcohol, or medicines, to be able to live their life? Some of you might say this is due to the pressure they have, and yes, that might be true, but do you think these people are thrilled from the inside?

I am pretty sure they aren't.

Their whole life is recorded, their bad days and emotions are visible online, and everybody is talking about them if they make a mistake. I am 100% convinced that all the money, the fame and the luxuries they have do not make them any happier, than people who have less money but are therefore satisfied from their inner self. Yes, money is essential, and yes, it also takes away pressure from your shoulders, if you do not need to look after every expense, but it doesn't necessarily make you happier.

In fact, successful people need to learn the ability to be convinced of themselves. It would be best if you were confident that your actions and your doings are right, that you have a good feeling about them.

Another vital thing to understand is that every successful person has a plan. I know that some people do not have any plan of where they want to go, is it a relationship, a job or a hobby, but believe me, you need to have goals. It would be best if you had achievable milestones. Whenever I work, or I am studying or writing on this book, I have a clear understanding of where I want to go. I set myself the goal to finish this or that within tomorrow evening, or by the end of the month, I want to be that far on my path. It is crucial to know where you go.

The airplane example at the beginning of this chapter explained why; if you set no goals and have no plans, you will end up somewhere you most likely didn't want to be.

Success also might change goals, and plans might change, as you move on in your life and go further on your path. Success goals might also shift in age. Right now you might think that having a lot of money is the main goal, after your marriage the main goal might be to have an excellent working family life, and as soon as you retire, your main goal might be to enjoy the last few years with your nearest ones. Goals change, and that is nothing bad, it just shows you, what is the most essential thing in your life, at every stage of your life. This is also part of setting priorities.

Is your priority to go partying every evening during your 20s, or is it to build up a company? Is it to have a stable job, where you earn enough to maintain your lifestyle or is to build up a family early? Whatever it is, you will find out where your priorities lie. Your priorities will show you the way but remember to listen to your heart and your feelings. If you don't feel like you want to go out tonight, you don't feel like it – stay at home. If you don't feel like you want to build up a company, then go and find a job. Whatever it is, it is your priority and your goal, and you should listen to what your body is telling you what to do.

Learn to take all the responsibility for your life on your own shoulders. We humans are very good in blaming our failure, or situation which didn't work out, on other people.

- I couldn't be there on time, because the tube was too slow. NO, you could have gone earlier. – Because my colleague was too slow with the report, the manager wasn't happy, NO, you could have helped your colleague deliver on time. My company failed, because I didn't have enough time, NO, set your priorities and you would have had enough time.

These are only a few examples, of how we always blame somebody or something else on our failures. However, setting the priorities in the right way will help you to understand that you are the person who could have changed it, other than blaming the others on your situation. Additionally, blaming others is giving your valuable energy to something, which will not help you on your further way. Use the experiences to move on, to achieve, and to follow your path into your inner success.

What are you giving back? Are you generous with the people around you?

See, success doesn't always mean that you, as a person, are getting successful in whatever you want to achieve. Success means to get to a point where you can also contribute to the world, to the people around you and to the whole society. Would you say that getting one bottle of plastic out of the ocean before it drowns is a success? Would you say that only selling one of your products is a success? Would you say that having a wonderful day with your family is a success?

I would. We need to understand that not only the big things can be counted as a success. Every contribution you are doing to this world, the people, nature, and your environment is a success in my eyes. Every small accomplishment you are doing is a success. We need to be thankful and proud of ourselves, to achieve small steps, to be able to celebrate the truly abundant final success we are working for.

What is your self-discipline? What are you doing all day long?

Everybody has 24 hours a day. If you are in London, New York or Shanghai, 24 hours is the time you get per day to achieve big. If you want to be successful, you need to understand that you need to do more than others throughout this day.

Let's imagine you sleep for seven hours, work for another eight hours, and daily travel for around two hours to get to your working place. If you do the math, you still have seven hours left every day. Of course, you are going to eat something and spend time with your family, friends or partner, but all in all, you will still have time left throughout every of your day. Are you scrolling through Facebook during this time, or are you reading something which will help you on your way towards success? Are you watching a TV show or series or are you watching a documentary, which gives you knowledge? Are you looking at dog videos on YouTube, or are you working on your next launch?

I think you see where I am going.

Yes, success requires hard work which comes with self-discipline. Yes, it is proven that social media is very distracting on your concentration. Yes, it is even proven that only having your phone next to you on the table while working, is distracting you from your work. You need to build self-discipline throughout your day to day life to achieve your goals. Think about a sportsman or sportswoman who has achieved significantly in their life. They all have self-discipline and work on themselves day by day. If you are working for financial success, social success, or on your relationship, you can directly also relate it to that. Constant work, self-discipline, and pure concentration and focus on your success will bring you there. Self-discipline also comes with self-development. Are you developing yourself? Are you reading, watching, or informing yourself about something that will bring you further in life?

It is essential to work on yourself, not only in the outside. The inside of each of us, our heart and our soul, is the most important thing we need to work on. We need to develop our self-love, our dedication, and our strengths, to achieve big. We also need to learn knowledge. We need to read about success, about careers and about the failure to have a clearer understanding of where we are going. It is super important to learn every day and to work every day for your purpose in life. There is a saying, that if you invest every day only one hour, only one hour of the seven hours you have left every day, that you will be a professional in the area you investigated after one year. This is 365 hours you invest to be a real professional, to have a clear understanding of what you are learning, and it only requires one hour a day.

Having a clear plan, a structure, and a goal will lead you to your success. It needs hard work and discipline, but I am undoubtedly sure that you are a person who can achieve big. You bought this book, not because you were bored, or are not interested in changing something in your life. I am sure you are interested, you are humble, and you are a personality who can work and make your dreams come true!

You might ask yourself the question; is success

really what I am searching for in life? Did I not already find my success?

Fortunately, scientists found out that success is not the most crucial thing in life anymore. Yes, you read correctly; it is happiness. Nowadays we are more and more concentrated on actual happiness in life, where success is a consequent of that. It is not anymore about hustling your ass off; it is more about being happy and finding your success within the process of living a happy life. I think that this way of thinking we nowadays have something great and that we should go on living in this mindset.

On the other hand, I am convinced that success includes hard work, hustle, early mornings and late nights, whereas I think that the young generations only think about how they would like to be happy and therefore having success, other than actually working for it. I got to know many people throughout my life who told me they would like to do this or that, that they have a plan and are working for it. Unfortunately, the dream and the energy invested in it was gone pretty quickly, as we still miss the impact we are striving for. I think that everybody should find their way of living the success and finding the path towards the real purpose in life. I want you also to know that it will not fly down from heaven. It requires constant work and dedication, and it is a process which requires patience. Overnight millionaires are very uncommon, and you should definitely not try to be one of them. Go your own way, and you will find what is best for you and your future life. I believe in you!

You are ready to be happy and successful!

Dear Reader,

Thank you from the bottom of my heart for reading my book;
"Change it! The secrets of happiness & fulfillment through change!"
It means a lot to me, to share my knowledge, and to bring you to the
next level of your life!

I am sure that you are on the right way of changing your life towards
success, happiness, and fulfillment!

I am working on future events and seminars, where I will further help
you and your business to grow to live your full potential, that's my
calling, and my purpose on this world and I am more than happy, that
you are part of this community!

If you would like to hear more about me and my upcoming events,
then please follow the following link!

www.amadeuslombardi.com

THANK YOU!

⟨ ⟩ @amadeuslombardi

Are you looking for an environmentally friendly fashion business?

**Welcome to my environmentally friendly
Fashion Label, SL.AM LDN!**

Through our highly professional designed hoodies, t-shirts,
leggings and many more goodies produced in Europe
through professionals, we want to show the world, how
our clothings are making a difference on this planet.

Our mission is to make the world a better place, by designing
and producing sustainable fashion; one clothing piece by SL.AM
LDN at a time will make our world a happy and clean planet.
Additionally, we want to raise awareness about social issues, which
include racism, LGBT and most importantly stereotypes.

These issues are something that still to this day take a huge
negative role, since it is the 21st century many would think that
everyone has achieved their growth mind-set where everyone
is accepting of one another however, there are still some minds
that have been constricted to a point that not even their minds
have changed the slightest with our changing world today.

It is time to accept one another no matter of their beliefs or
who they are because everyone is unique in their own way and
we hope to create a community of togetherness. A community
loving and accepting of one another and where no one has
to live in fear of being judged by anyone ever again.

Our vision is to create a world which is non-stereotyped
and a world which is accepting, understanding and
loving, with an environmental situation, which is showing
itself in pure beauty and natural refinement.

It is time for change.

Welcome to SL.AM LDN, the fashion label of tomorrow.

LDN

Check it out under www.slamldn.com   Instagram: @sl.amldn

Lightning Source UK Ltd.
Milton Keynes UK
UKHW011313170220
358851UK00004B/1485